JAZZ SUITE

HORN I

I
Horns O'Plenty

Alec Wilder

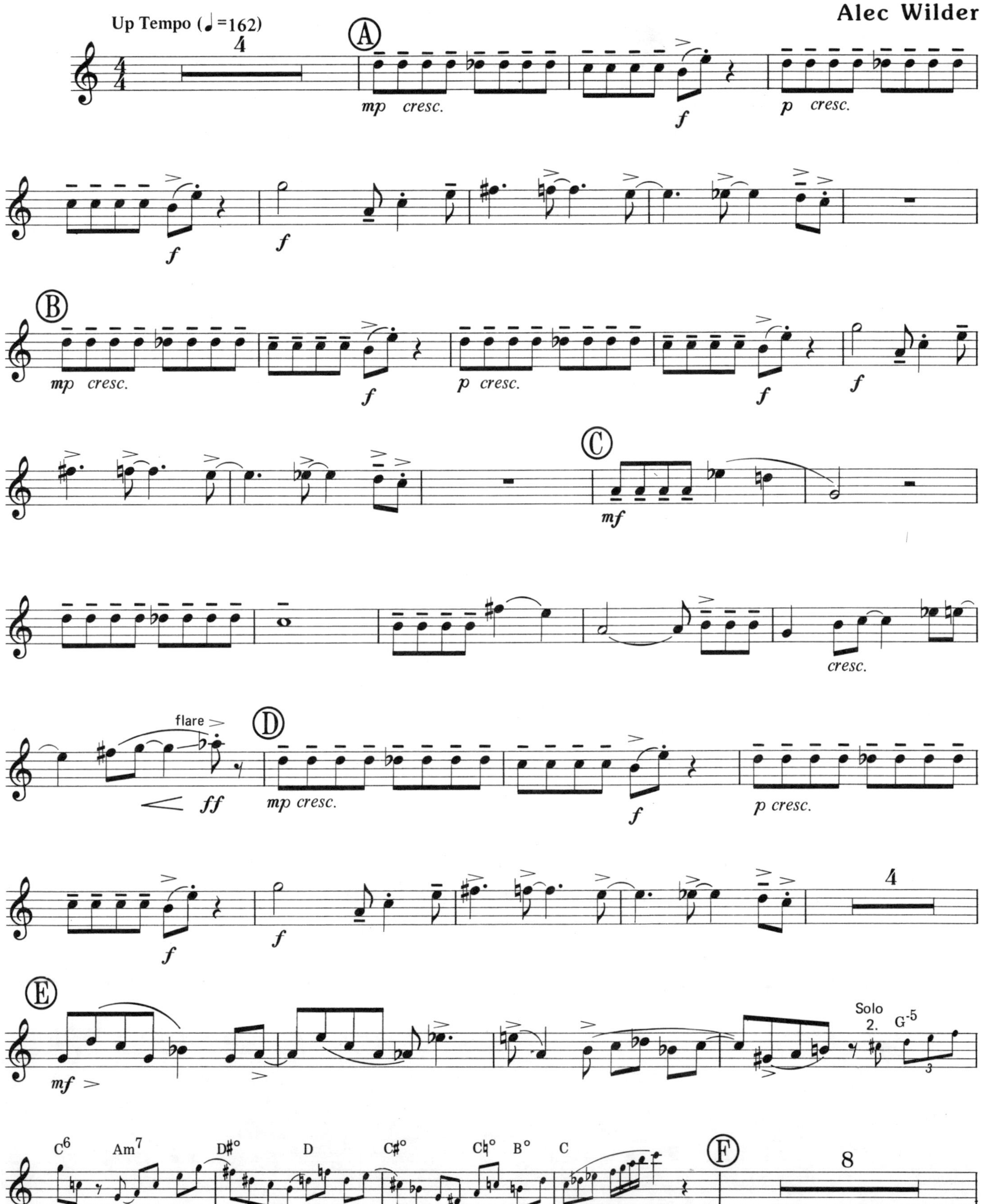

Up Tempo (♩=162)

4

Ⓐ

mp cresc. f p cresc. f f

Ⓑ

mp cresc. f p cresc. f f

Ⓒ

mf

cresc.

flare

Ⓓ

ff mp cresc. f p cresc. f f

4

Ⓔ

mf

Solo 2. G-5

C6 Am7 D♯° D C♯° C♮° B° C

Ⓕ

8

G smear smear H poco f marc. J flare flare K L f dim. mp pp f sub. even rip ff

II
Conversation Piece

Medium Tempo (♩=126)

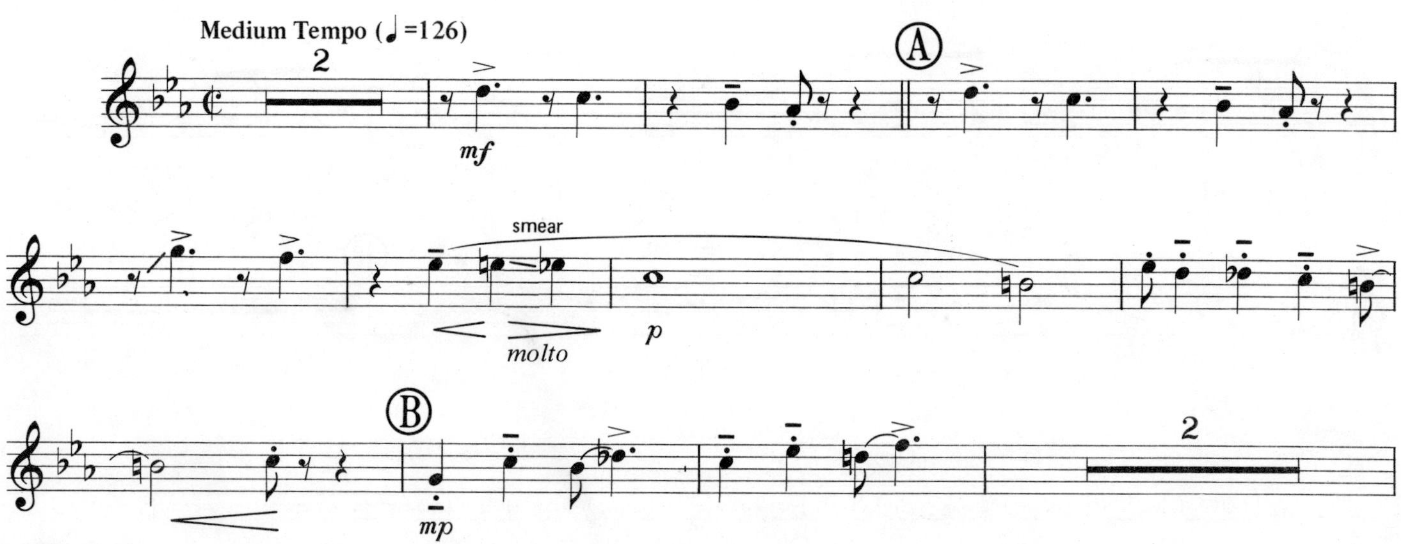

C
D
E
F
G
H
J
mp
mf
p
f
fp
ff

III
Serenade

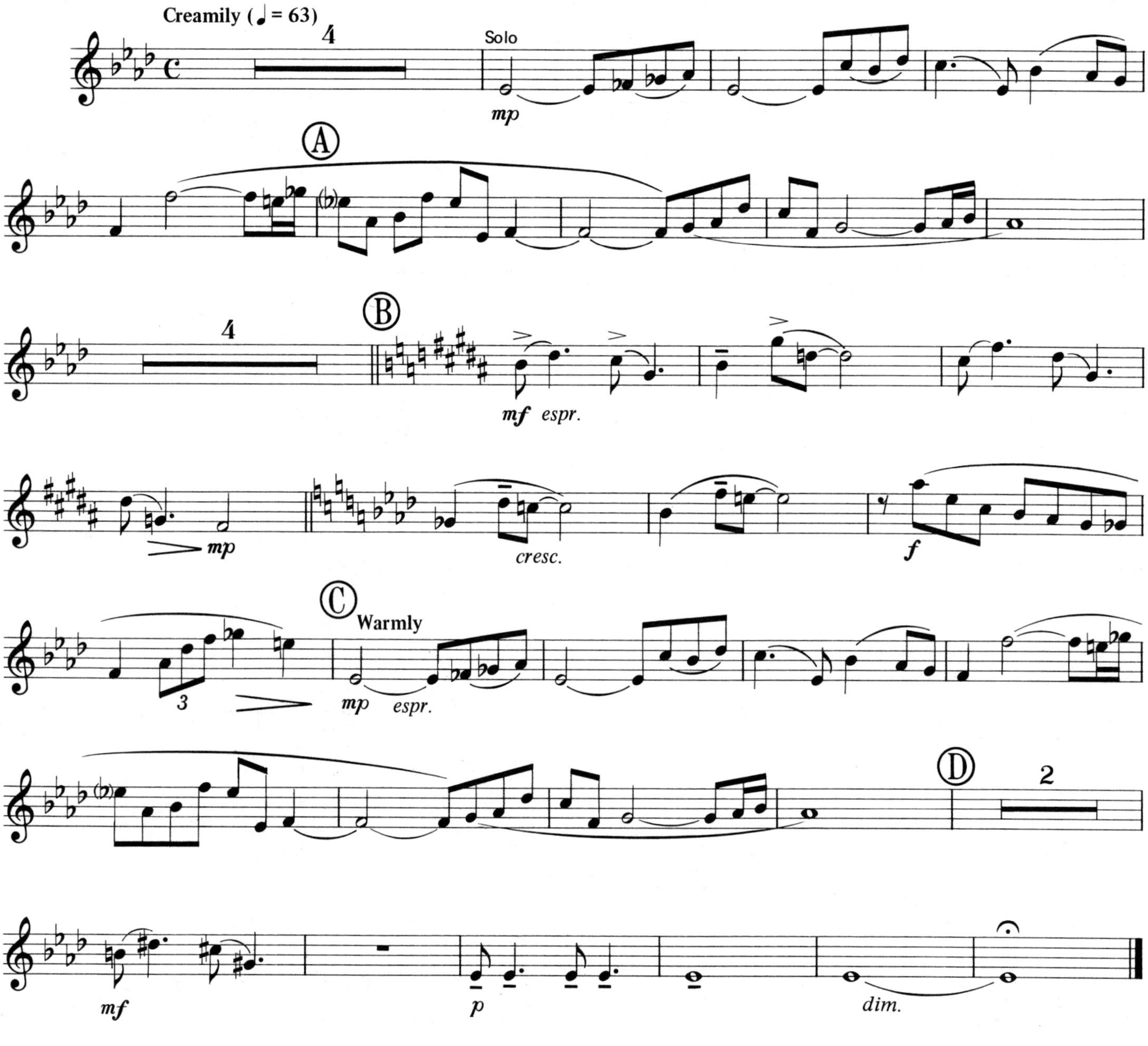

Creamily (♩ = 63)
4
Solo
mp
A
B
4
mf espr.
mp
cresc.
f
C
Warmly
3
mp espr.
D
2
mf
p
dim.

IV
Horn Belt Boogie

Fast (♩ =168)
2
mf
3
A
(Soft-tongued)
3
p
f
B
10
mf p
f

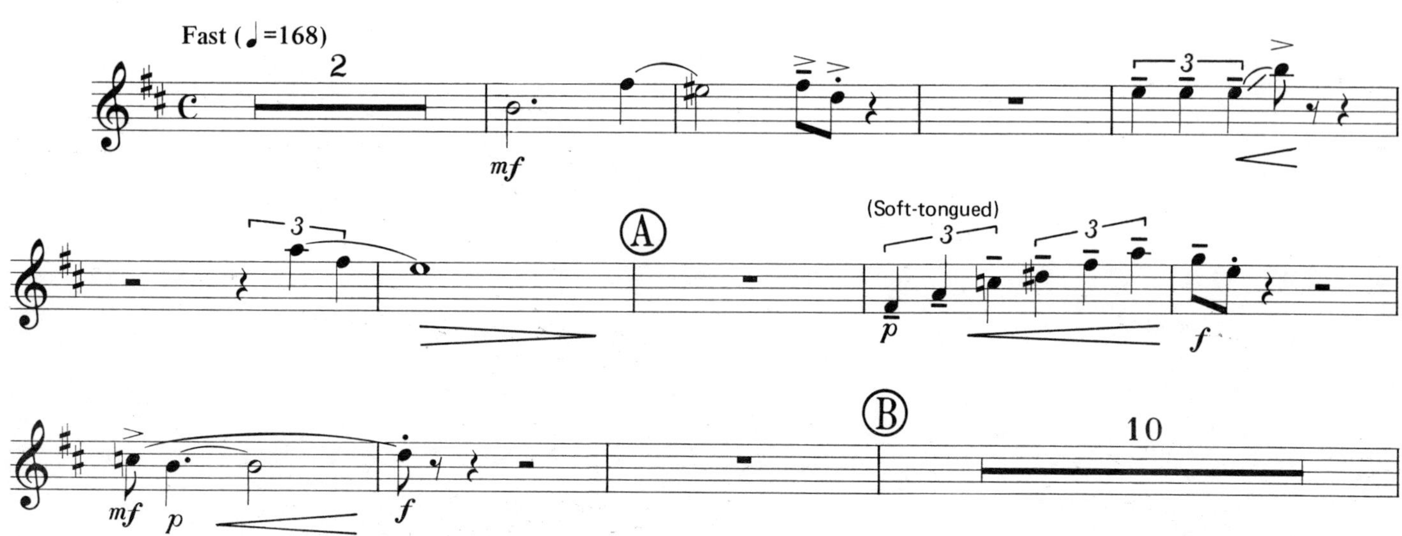

C
flare
sim.
D
Solo
2.
E
4
F
G
H
J
f
ff
fmp
mf
mp
p
dim.

Other ensemble and solo music of interest to brass players from Margun

J.S. Bach

Chorale (from *Cantata No. 60*)
set by Gunther Schuller for two trumpets, horn and trombone
One of Bach's most extraordinary chorales and harmonic inventions; used by Alban Berg in his Violin Concerto

J.S. Bach

Prelude No. 22 (from *Well-Tempered Clavier*)
set by Gunther Schuller for two trumpets, two horns and two trombones
One of the highlights of Bach's well-known masterpiece; the key of B-flat minor inspired Bach to some truly incredible harmonic flights which sound even more dramatic on brass instruments

Brass Transcriptions – Trios, quartets, quintets, sextets and septets (comprising trumpet, horn and trombone) by various 15th- and 16th-century composers, set by Gunther Schuller
Brass transcriptions in a variety of ensemble combinations ranging from motets and madrigals by Dufay, Gesualdo and Marenzio to DeRore's profoundly moving Latin Ode (for four trombones)

Louis Dauprat

Sextuor No. 1 for six horns
A brilliant virtuoso excursion for six horns by the Paris Conservatoire's first professor of horn, appointed by no less than Napoleon; great fun to play, range from low C to high g (concert)

Avram David

Sonata, op. 101 for solo horn
A challenging, almost heroic tour-de-force for unaccompanied horn–ingeniously composed so as not to kill off the horn player–by the well-known Boston-based composer

Lucia Dlugoszewski

Space Is a Diamond for solo trumpet
A remarkable exploration of the outer reaches of trumpet technique; composed for and recorded by Gerard Schwarz; published in a handsome, multi-color engraved edition

Tibor Pusztai

Interactions for horn and three percussion
Effective three-movement work for solo horn set against a diverse percussion background

Gunther Schuller

Fanfare for four trumpets and four trombones
A short, functional 1½-minute fanfare in a harmonic style somewhat akin to Messiaen

Perpetuum Mobile for four muted horns and bassoon (or tuba)
A light-hearted bagatelle in the manner of a Poulenc or Bozza

Trois Hommages for horn(s) and piano
1. À Frederick Delius 2. À Maurice Ravel 3. À Darius Milhaud
Early vintage Schuller, dedicated to three of his youthful influences; accessible, attractive recital and teaching pieces

Robert Selig

Variations for brass quintet
A challenging and difficult single-movement quintet by this dynamic Boston composer

Alec Wilder

Brass Quintets Nos. 1-8

Effie Joins a Carnival for tuba and brass quartet

Elegy for tuba and brass ensemble

Nonet for eight horns and tuba
One of Wilder's finest works: eight horns and tuba in four jazz settings

Sonata for bass trombone and piano

Suites Nos. 1-5 for tuba and piano

Suites Nos. 1 & 2 for horn, tuba and piano

Ellen Taaffe Zwilich

Clarino Quartet for piccolo trumpet, D trumpet and two B-flat trumpets
Brilliant tour-de-force for trumpets in three movements; range from low F to high f (concert)

JAZZ SUITE

HORN II

I
Horns O'Plenty

Alec Wilder

II
Conversation Piece

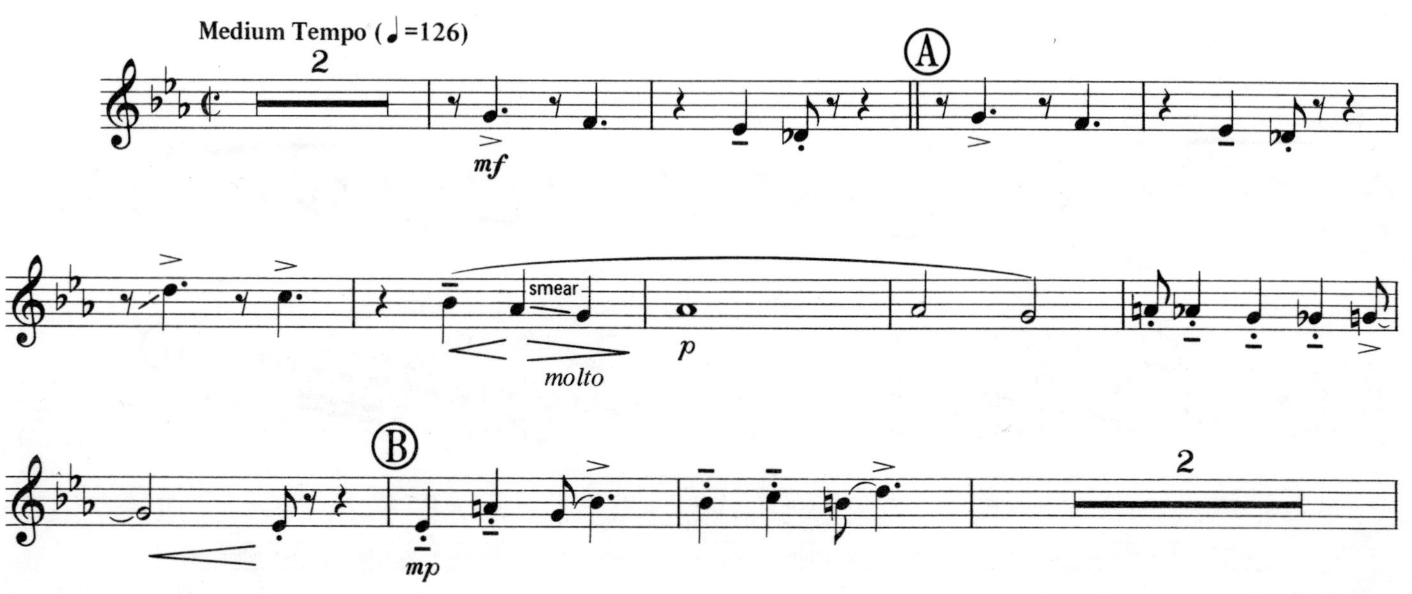

C
D
E
F
G
H
J

III
Serenade
Creamily (♩ = 63)
mp
p
sim.
A
espr.
B
4
sfz (poco)
mf espr.
cresc.
C
Warmly
mf
mp espr.
D
2
dim.
IV
Horn Belt Boogie
Fast (♩ = 168)
2
mf
3
A
(Soft-tongued)
f
B
10
mf p
C
ff
flare
f mp

sim.
Solo
D
E
F
G
H
J
4
dim.

Other ensemble and solo music of interest to brass players from Margun

J.S. Bach

Chorale (from *Cantata No. 60)*
set by Gunther Schuller for two trumpets, horn and trombone
One of Bach's most extraordinary chorales and harmonic inventions; used by Alban Berg in his Violin Concerto

J.S. Bach

Prelude No. 22 (from *Well-Tempered Clavier*)
set by Gunther Schuller for two trumpets, two horns and two trombones
One of the highlights of Bach's well-known masterpiece; the key of B-flat minor inspired Bach to some truly incredible harmonic flights which sound even more dramatic on brass instruments

Brass Transcriptions – Trios, quartets, quintets, sextets and septets (comprising trumpet, horn and trombone) by various 15th- and 16th-century composers, set by Gunther Schuller
Brass transcriptions in a variety of ensemble combinations ranging from motets and madrigals by Dufay, Gesualdo and Marenzio to DeRore's profoundly moving Latin Ode (for four trombones)

Louis Dauprat

Sextuor No. 1 for six horns
A brilliant virtuoso excursion for six horns by the Paris Conservatoire's first professor of horn, appointed by no less than Napoleon; great fun to play, range from low C to high g (concert)

Avram David

Sonata, op. 101 for solo horn
A challenging, almost heroic tour-de-force for unaccompanied horn–ingeniously composed so as not to kill off the horn player–by the well-known Boston-based composer

Lucia Dlugoszewski

Space Is a Diamond for solo trumpet
A remarkable exploration of the outer reaches of trumpet technique; composed for and recorded by Gerard Schwarz; published in a handsome, multi-color engraved edition

Tibor Pusztai

Interactions for horn and three percussion
Effective three-movement work for solo horn set against a diverse percussion background

Gunther Schuller

Fanfare for four trumpets and four trombones
A short, functional 1½-minute fanfare in a harmonic style somewhat akin to Messiaen

Perpetuum Mobile for four muted horns and bassoon (or tuba)
A light-hearted bagatelle in the manner of a Poulenc or Bozza

Trois Hommages for horn(s) and piano
1. À Frederick Delius 2. À Maurice Ravel 3. À Darius Milhaud
Early vintage Schuller, dedicated to three of his youthful influences; accessible, attractive recital and teaching pieces

Robert Selig

Variations for brass quintet
A challenging and difficult single-movement quintet by this dynamic Boston composer

Alec Wilder

Brass Quintets Nos. 1-8

Effie Joins a Carnival for tuba and brass quartet

Elegy for tuba and brass ensemble

Nonet for eight horns and tuba
One of Wilder's finest works: eight horns and tuba in four jazz settings

Sonata for bass trombone and piano

Suites Nos. 1-5 for tuba and piano

Suites Nos. 1 & 2 for horn, tuba and piano

Ellen Taaffe Zwilich

Clarino Quartet for piccolo trumpet, D trumpet and two B-flat trumpets
Brilliant tour-de-force for trumpets in three movements; range from low F to high f (concert)

HORN III

Alec Wilder

JAZZ SUITE

for Horn Quartet, Harpsichord, Guitar, Bass and Drums

I. Horns O'Plenty
II. Conversation Piece
III. Serenade
IV. Horn Belt Boogie

MARGUN MUSIC INC.

167 Dudley Road Newton Centre Massachusetts 02159

JAZZ SUITE

I
Horns O'Plenty

HORN III

Alec Wilder

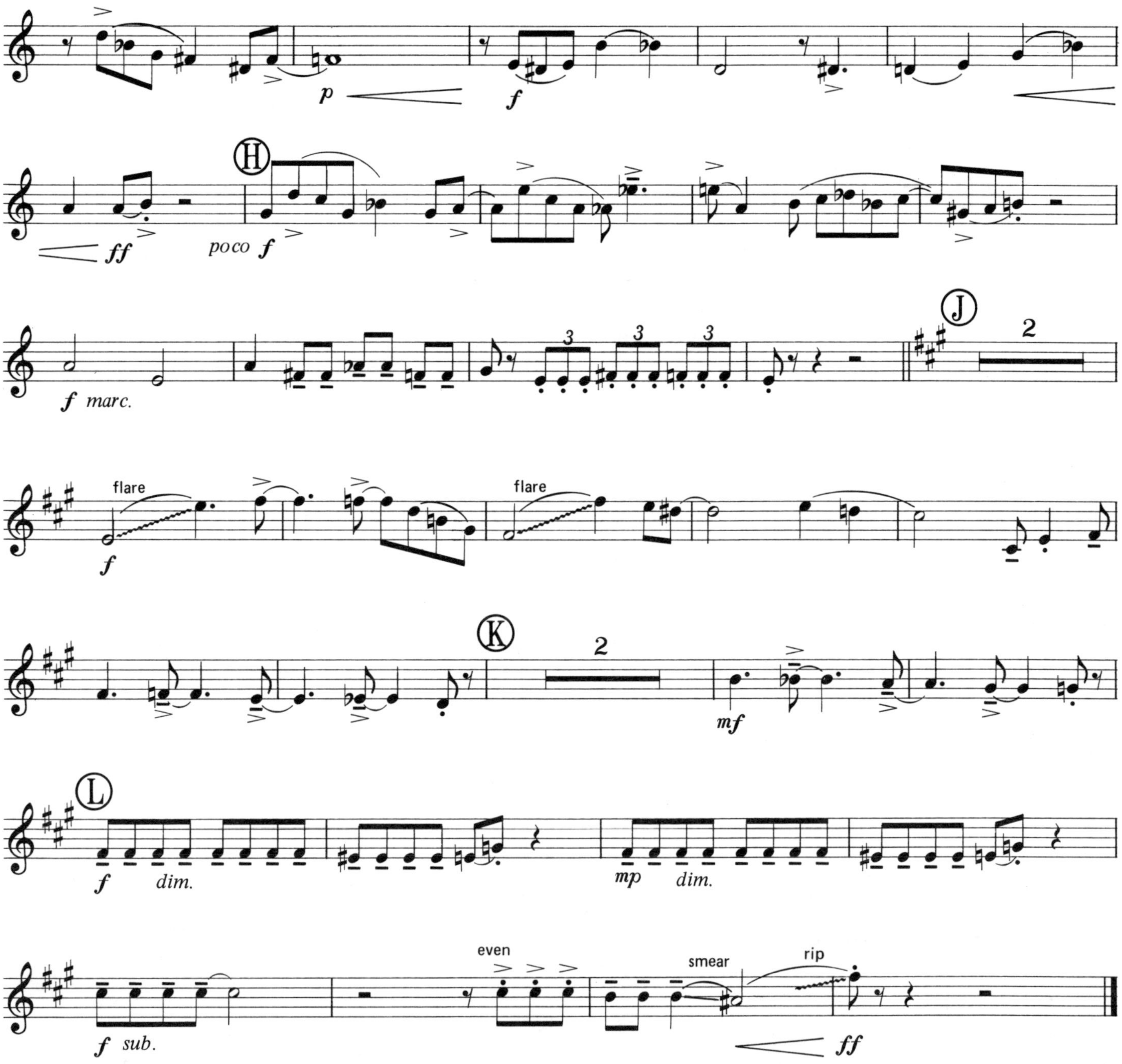

p f ff poco f H f marc. J 2 flare f flare K 2 mf L f dim. mp dim. f sub. even smear rip ff

II
Conversation Piece

Medium Tempo (♩ = 126)

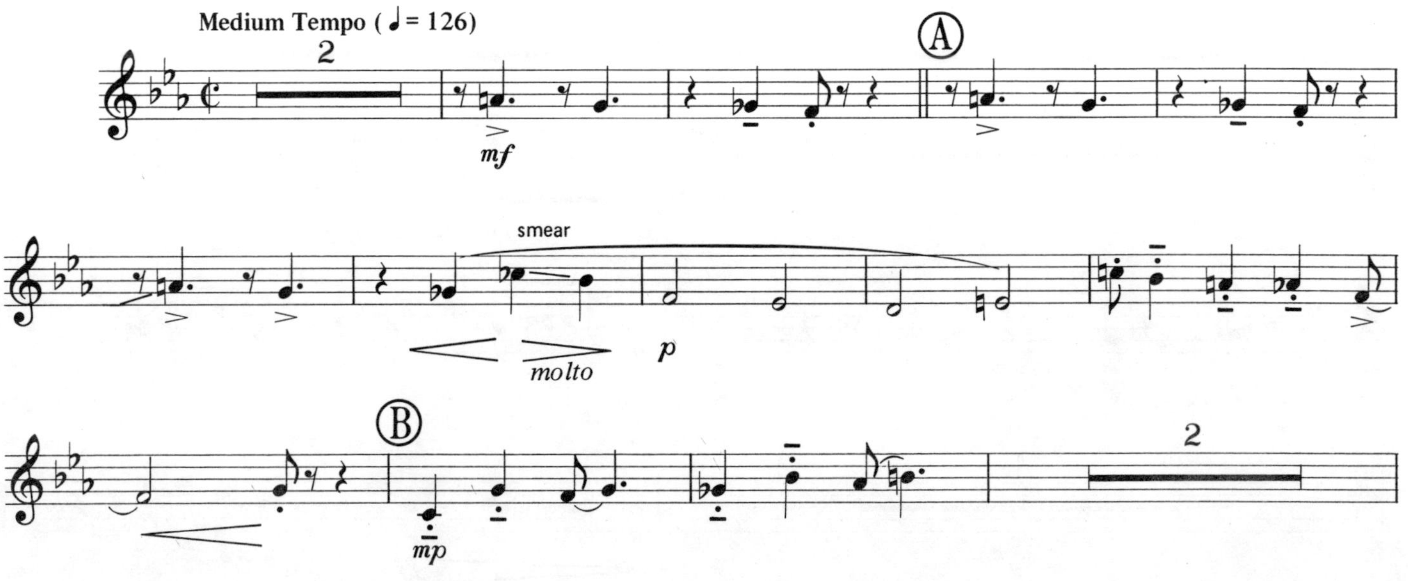

mp
mf
2
C
mf
mf
mf
D
6
mf
E
2
mf
2
mf
F
p
f
mf
fp
G
mf
mf
p
H
2
mf
2
mf
fp
f
J
f
f
4
f
ff

III
Serenade

Creamily (♩ = 63)

mp mp mp mp mp mp mp mp p p

sim.

A

p

B

4

sfz (poco)

p p

mf espr.

mp

cresc.

mf

C Warmly

mp espr.

D

2

mf

p

dim.

IV
Horn Belt Boogie

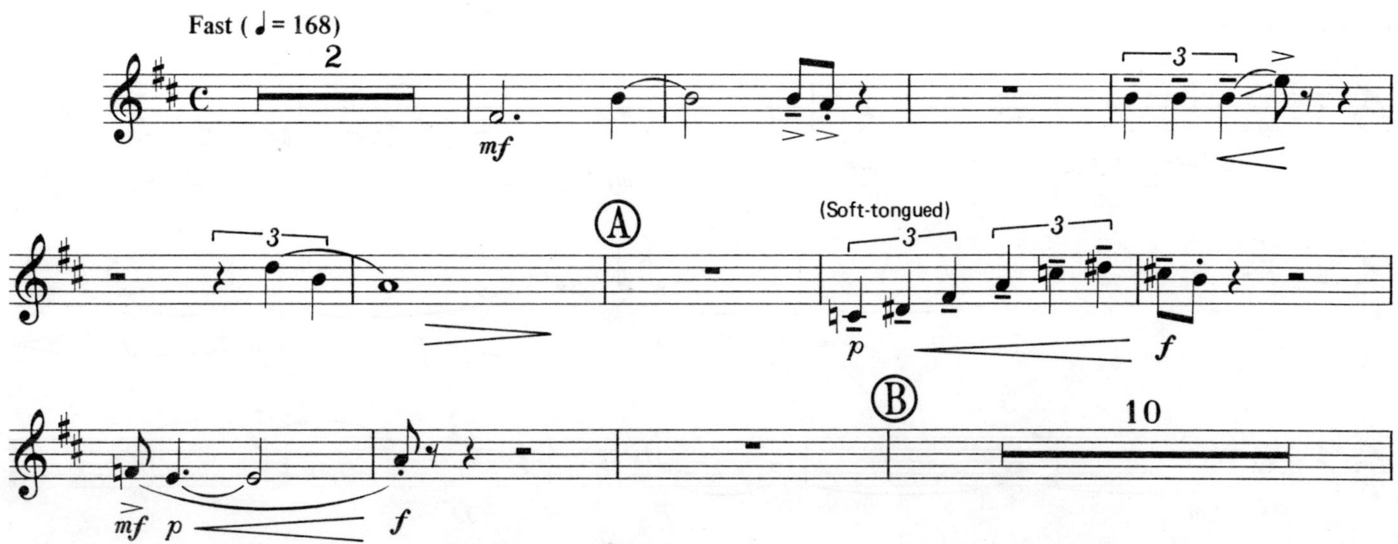

C
flare
sim.
D
E
11
F
4
G
H
J
dim.

HORN IV

Alec Wilder

JAZZ SUITE

for Horn Quartet, Harpsichord, Guitar, Bass and Drums

I. Horns O'Plenty
II. Conversation Piece
III. Serenade
IV. Horn Belt Boogie

MARGUN MUSIC INC.

167 Dudley Road Newton Centre Massachusetts 02159

JAZZ SUITE

I
Horns O'Plenty

HORN IV

Alec Wilder

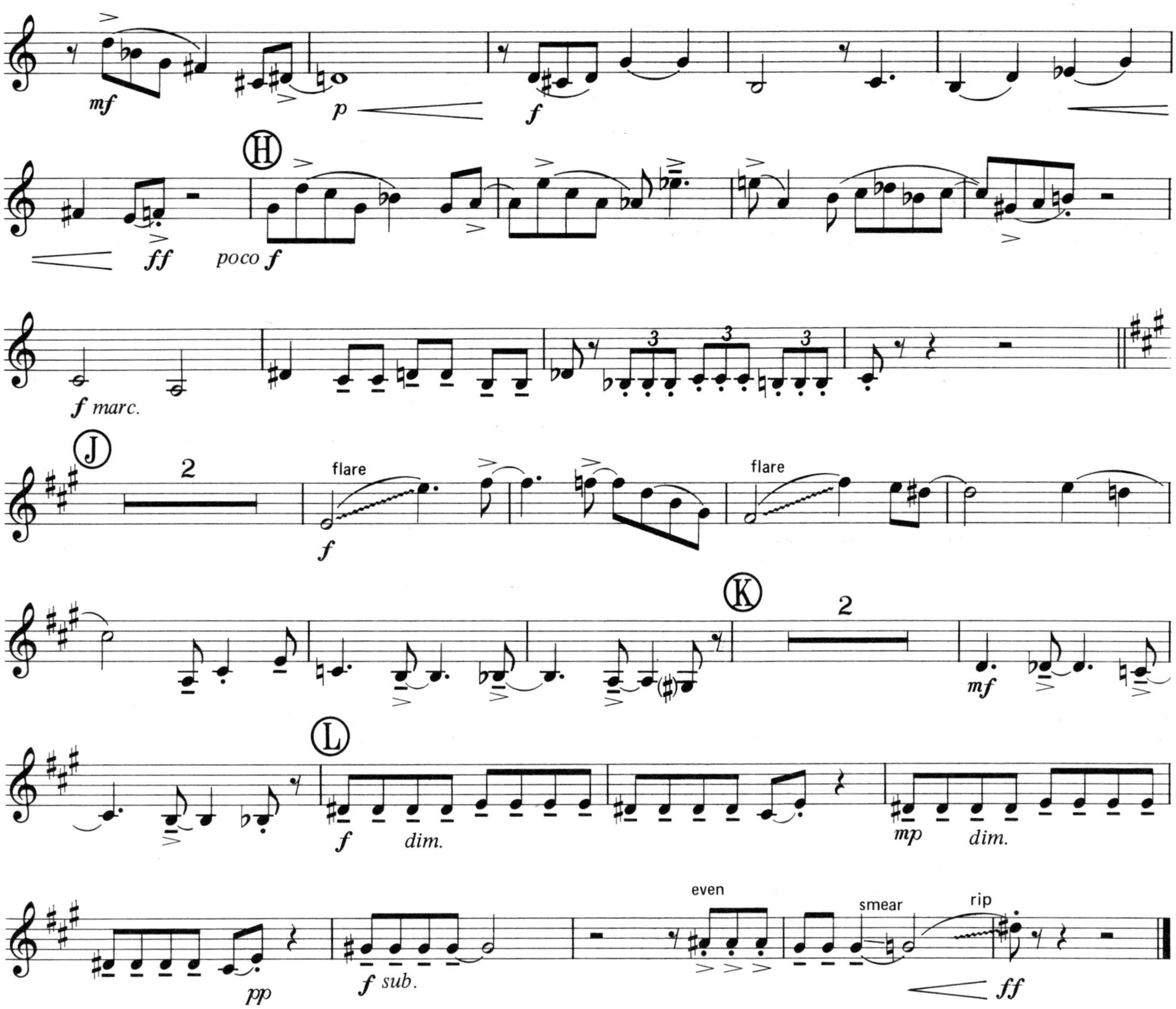

mf
p
f
H
ff
poco f
f marc.
J
2
flare
f
flare
K
2
mf
L
f
dim.
mp
dim.
pp
f sub.
even
smear
rip
ff

II
Conversation Piece

Medium Tempo (♩ = 126) 2
mf
A
smear
molto
p
B
mp
2
mp
3
3
3
3
mf
2

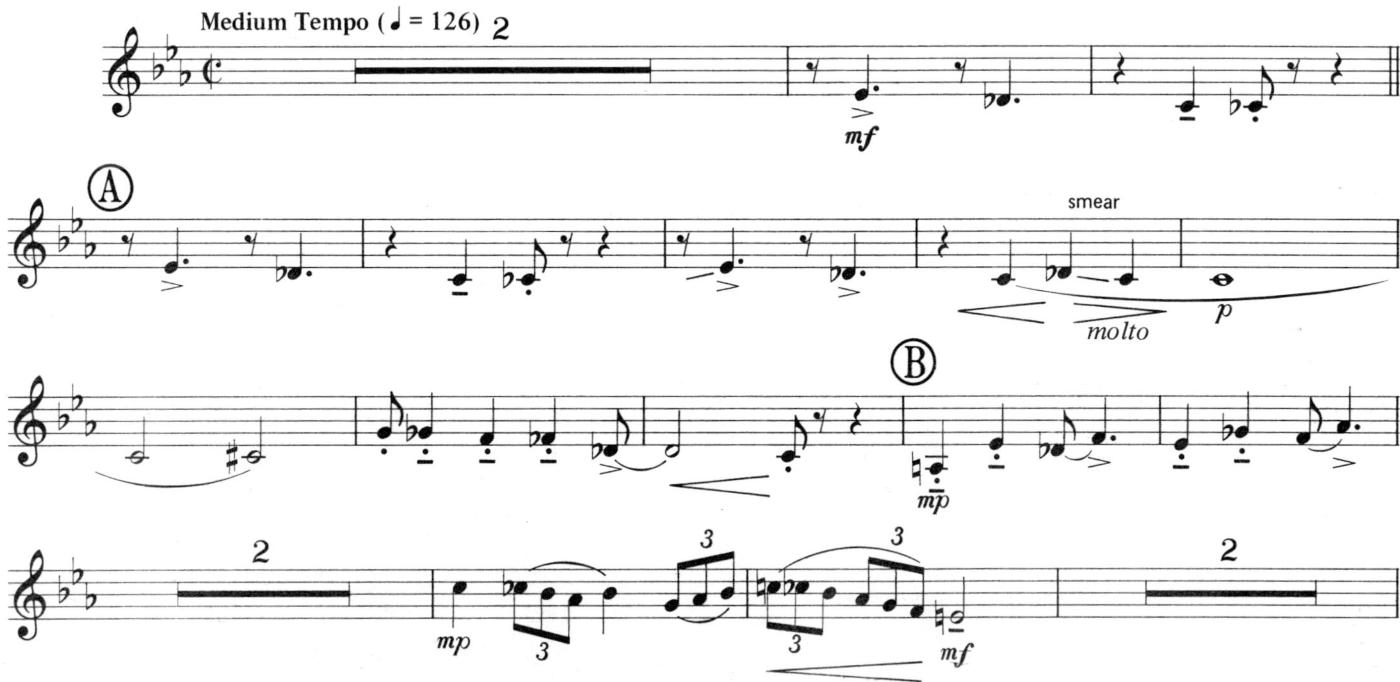

C
mf
mf
mf
D
6
mf
E
6
mf
(sounds 5th lower)
F
p
f
mf
fp
G
mf
mf
H
4
2
mf
fp
f
J
f
f
4
f
ff

III
Serenade

Creamily (♩ = 63)

mp mp mp mp mp mp mp mp p p

sim.

A

p

4

B

sfz (poco) p p mf espr.

cresc.

mp mf

C Warmly

mp espr.

D 2

mf p dim.

IV
Horn Belt Boogie

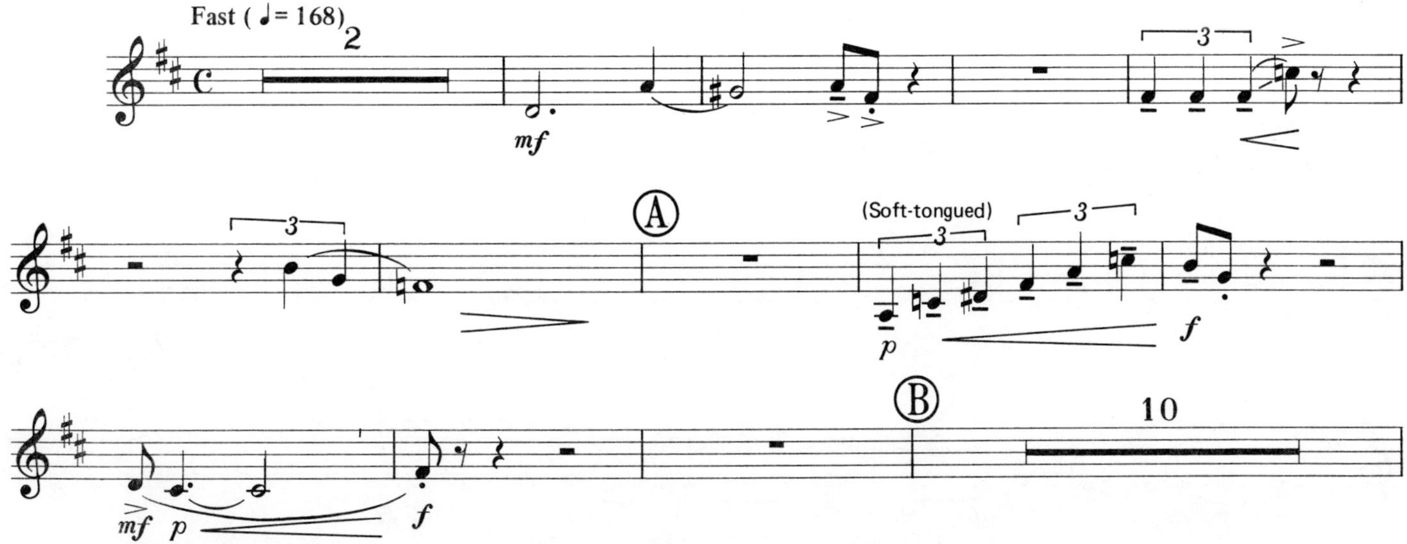

C
f
ff
f
flare
fmp
sim.
f
fmp
f
f
D
3
ff
mf
E
11
F
ff
f
4
G
fmp
mf
3
f
ff
3
f
mp
3
3
f
H
f
ff
ff
mf
mf
mf
J
ff
p
f
p
f
mf dim.
p
ff

JAZZ SUITE

I

Horns O'Plenty

HARPSICHORD

Alec Wilder

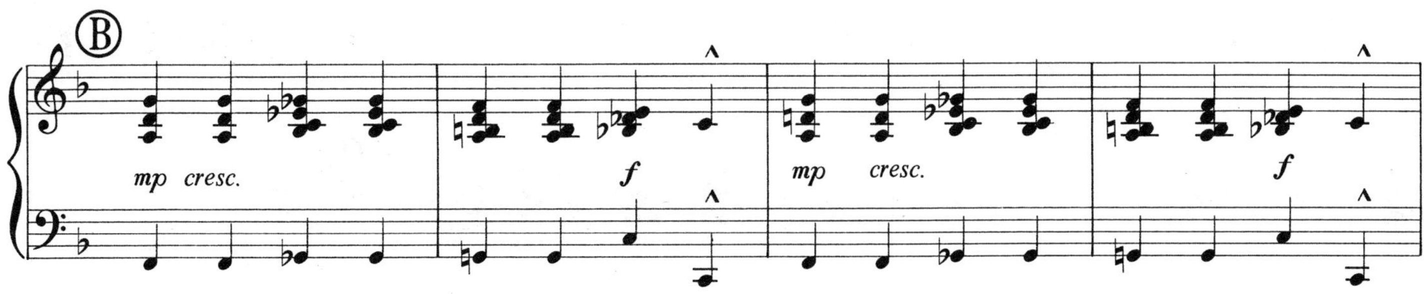

C
mf
fill in
fill in
cresc.
ff
D
mp cresc.
f
mp cresc.
f
f
E
mf

F
f
F6 Ebm(6)
G9 C7(-9/-5)
F6 Ebm(6)
G-9 C7(-9/-5)
F(6) Dm7
E-9 A-9
D-9 G-9 C-9
F F7
G
f 3
ff
H
mf
f
f 3 3 3

J
ad lib. accomp.
D
Cm6
E9
E♭-9
D6
Cm6

E9
E -9

K
(ad lib.)
f

L
f dim. poco a poco
pp
pp

(even)
f sub.
ff

II
Conversation Piece

Medium Tempo (♩ = 126)

D
Solo
E
Solo
F
Solo
mf

G
Solo
H
J
2
f
f
ff

HARPSICHORD

III
Serenade

C
mp

D
f
mf
f

p

IV
Horn Belt Boogie

Fast (♩= 168)

C
f
D
E
ad lib.

ff
F
f
f
3
3
3
3
G

H
f
J
dim.
p
trem.
ff

Solo literature and chamber music of interest to the pianist from Margun

For Solo Piano

Jean Barraqué

Sonata (1952) 40'
Monumental landmark of contemporary piano literature; a major contribution to the post-war Webern-Messiaen legacy

Bruno Bartolozzi

Estri del fa diesis (1959) 9'
Fine contemporary piano writing; in eight sections: impulsive, tenderly, capricious, contemplative, amorous, enigmatic, impetuous, intense; all about F-sharp

Ran Blake

Third Stream Compositions (1955-1970)
Fascinating transcriptions of Third Stream's major pianist-composer-proselytizer; something *really* different

Avram David

Hommage to Marcel Duchamp, op. 49 (1976) 6'
A tribute to the great artist, utilizing the principle of *objets trouvês,* including a notated polyphonic rhythmicization of Duchamp's famous aleatoric 1913 composition, *Musical Erratum.*

Robert DiDomenica

Improvisations (1974) 12'
A substantial, four-movement work, in serial technique fused with jazz gestures and attitudes

Robert DiDomenica

Eleven Short Pieces (1973) 8'
Concise, distinctly individual movements, technically challenging; in cyclical format

Domenico Guaccero

Sonatina prima (1957) 10'
A three-movement sonata in modified serial style (of moderate difficulty); pupil of Petrassi

George Perle

Six Etudes (1973-76) 12'
A major contribution to contemporary piano literature; to our time what Debussy's *Etudes* were to his

Edward Steuermann

Suite (1950) 15'
A beautiful, expressive five-movement suite by this most underrated composer, pianist and close friend of Schönberg

Chamber Music

Robert DiDomenica

Quartet for flute, violin, horn and piano (1959) 12'
Sensitive, lyrical chamber music by this fine Boston-based composer-flutist-teacher

Robert DiDomenica

Sonata after Essays for piano, soprano, baritone, flute/alto flute and tape (1977) 35'
A major piano sonata inspired by Ives' ***Essays before a Sonata*** with secondary parts for the two singers, flutist and tape

Robert DiDomenica

Arrangements for chamber ensemble, soprano and tape (1979) 12'
A light, but not unserious three-movement work, exploring the diverse worlds of John Cage, Lester Young, Slam Stewart, Bartok and Goethe

William Thomas McKinley

Paintings No. 4 for flute/piccolo, clarinet, cello, piano and percussion (1979) 13'
A powerful, emotion-laden chamber ensemble work by this prolific Boston-based composer-teacher-jazz pianist; requires a conductor

Arnold Schönberg

Verklärte Nacht, arr. Edward Steuermann for violin, cello and piano (1899) 30'
An extraordinarily successful arrangement of Schönberg's classic by the pianist for whom he wrote all his piano works

Gunther Schuller

Curtain Raiser for flute, clarinet, horn and piano (1960) 2'
A playful miniature – accessible light ensemble music

Lewis Spratlan

Dance Suite for violin, clarinet, guitar and harpsichord (1973) 15'
A delightful contemporary romp through olden dance forms

Alec Wilder

Trio for violin, cello and piano 13'
One of Wilder's rare excursions into the string literature; easy, affable, delightful music

JAZZ SUITE

GUITAR

I
Horns O'Plenty

Alec Wilder

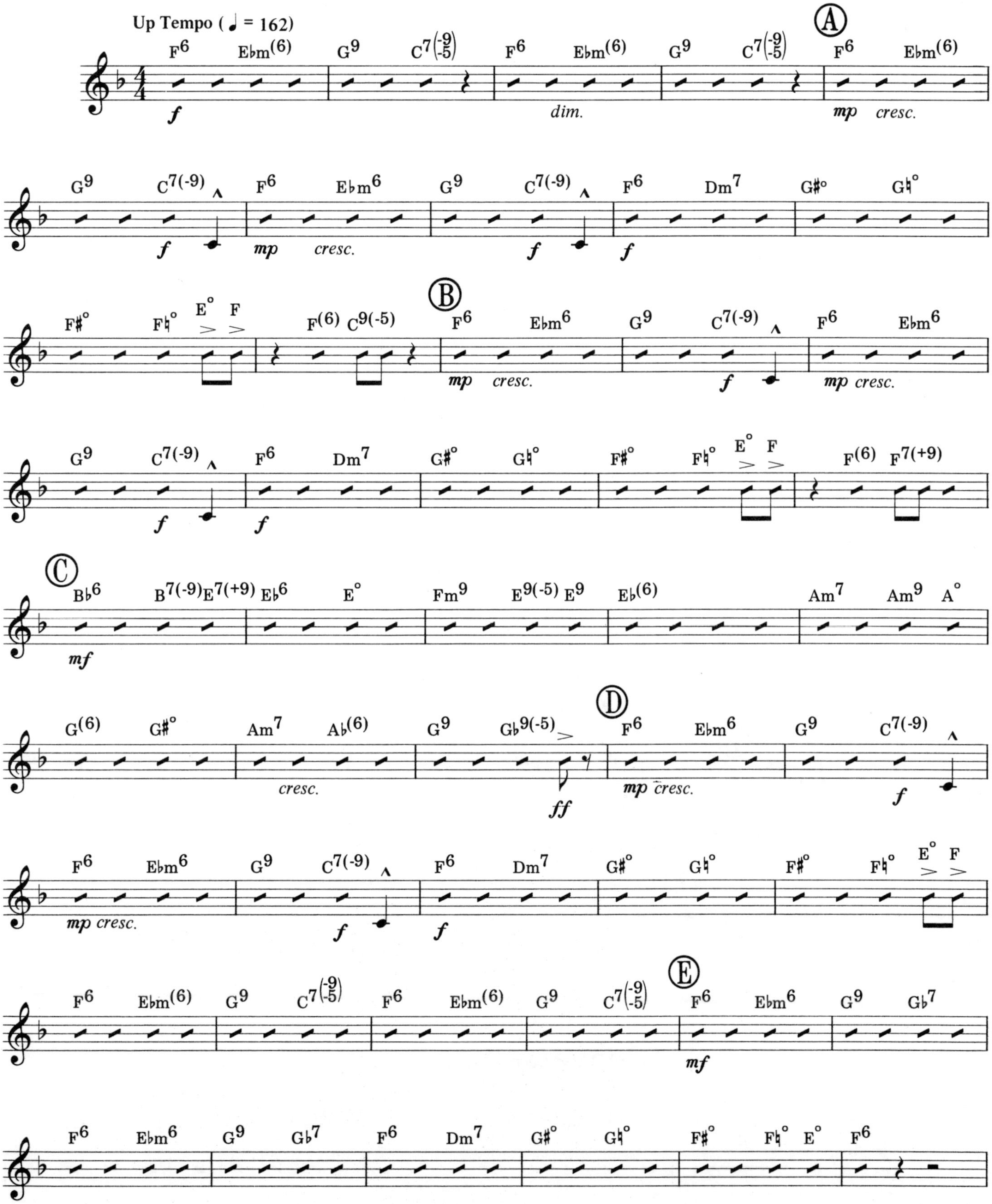

Up Tempo (♩ = 162)

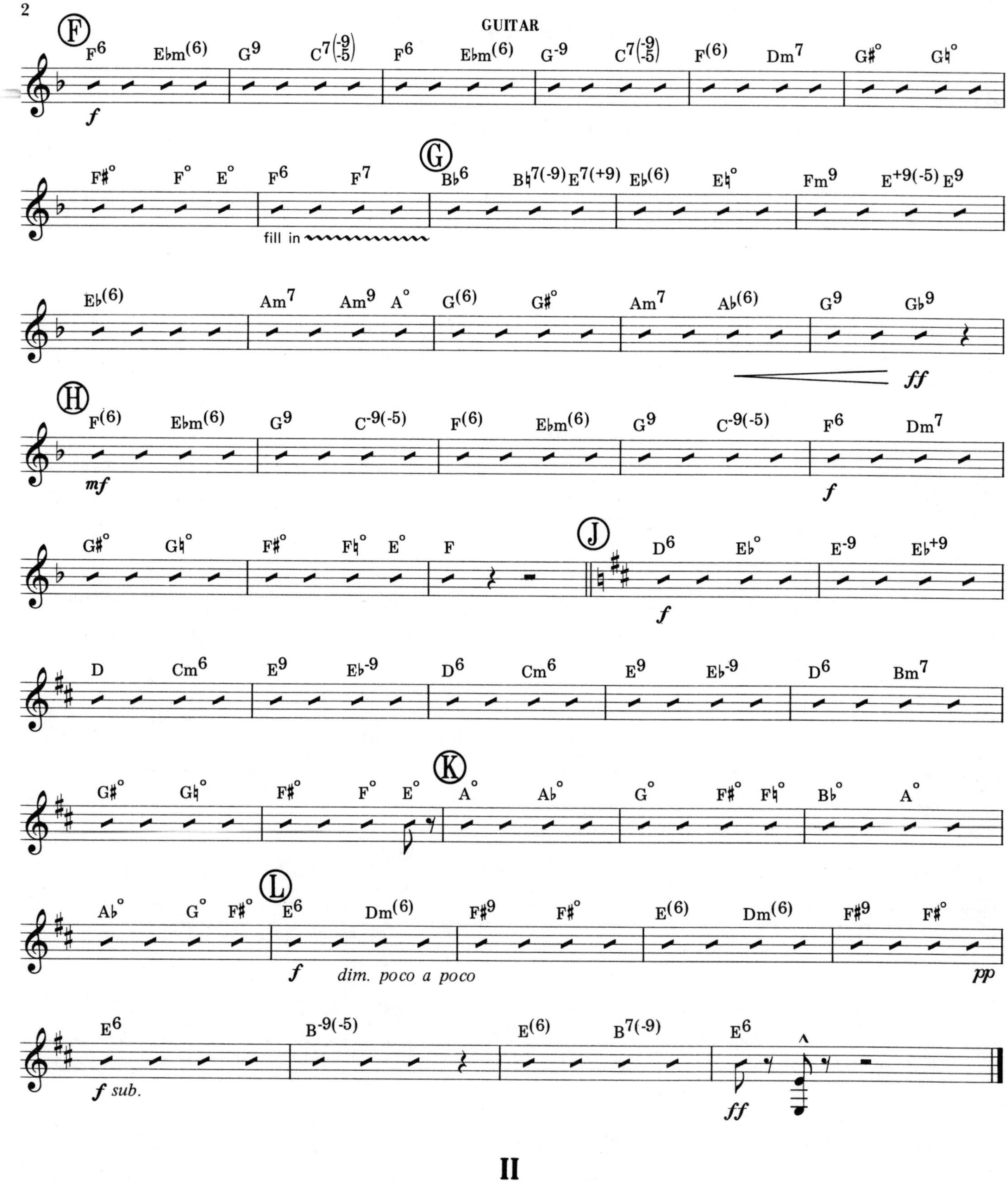

F
F6 Ebm(6) G9 C7(-9 -5) F6 Ebm(6) G-9 C7(-9 -5) F(6) Dm7 G#° G♮°
f
F#° F° E° F6 F7
G
Bb6 B♮7(-9) E7(+9) Eb(6) E♮° Fm9 E+9(-5) E9
fill in
Eb(6) Am7 Am9 A° G(6) G#° Am7 Ab(6) G9 Gb9
ff
H
F(6) Ebm(6) G9 C-9(-5) F(6) Ebm(6) G9 C-9(-5) F6 Dm7
mf
f
G#° G♮° F#° F♮° E° F
J
D6 Eb° E-9 Eb+9
f
D Cm6 E9 Eb-9 D6 Cm6 E9 Eb-9 D6 Bm7
G#° G♮° F#° F° E°
K
A° Ab° G° F#° F♮° Bb° A°
Ab° G° F#°
L
E6 Dm(6) F#9 F#° E(6) Dm(6) F#9 F#°
f
dim. poco a poco
pp
E6 B-9(-5) E(6) B7(-9) E6
f sub.
ff

II
Conversation Piece

2
Fm9(6) Ab9(6) Db9 Gb7
A
Fm9(6) Ab9(6) Db9 Gb7
mf
Fm9(6) Ab9(6) Db9 Gb7(+9) F7(+9) Bbm Bbm7 Bbm6 Am6 Fm(6) A9(-5) D9(-5) G9(-5) C7(-5)

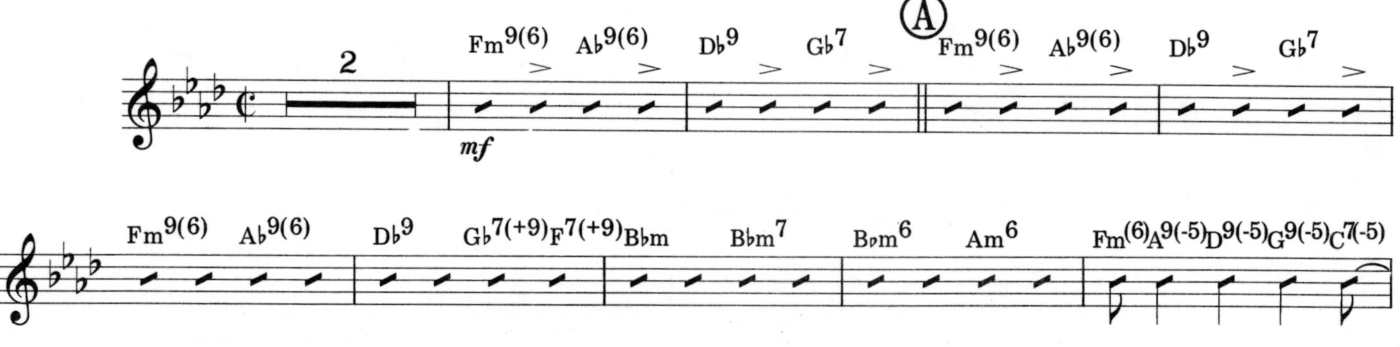

B
C7(-5) Fm
Fm(6) Ab9 Db9 G° Fm(6) Ab9 Db9 Bb° F7(+9)
mp
Bbm Bbm7 Bbm6 Am6 Fm(6) A9(-5) D9(-5) G9(-5) C7(-5) Fm
f
C
Bbm7 E♮m(6) E°
mf
Ab(6) Fm7 Em7 Am7 Ebm(6) G6 Ab G Gb F Bb9
Db9(-5) Dbm(6)
D
Fm Ab9 Db9 Db° C7(-9) Fm Ab9 Db9 Db° C°
Bbm Bbm7 Bbm6 Am6 Fm A9(-5) D9(-5) G9(-5) C7(-5) Fm
E
Dm F7 Bb9 Eb9 Eb9(-5) Dm F7(6) Bb7(6) Eb9 D7 Gm Gm7
Gm(6) F#m(6) Dm F#9 B+9 E9 Aaug9 Eb9(+5) Dm6
F
Dm F7 Bb7 Eb9(-5)
mp
Dm F9 Bb7 Eb9 D7 Gm Gm7 Gm(6) F#m(6) Dm F#9 Baug7 E9
Eb9(-5) Dm
G
Gm7 Dbm(6) Db° F6 Dm6 C#m7 F#m9 Baug-9 E6 C#m7
F E Eb D G9 Bb9 E7 Aaug7(-5)
H
Dm F7
Bb9 Eb9 Eb9(-5) Dm F7(6) Bb7(6) Eb9 D7 Gm Gm7 Gm(6) F#m(6)
Dm F#9 Baug7 E9 Eb9(-5) Dm Db7
J
Fm9(6) Ab9(6) Db9 Gb7(-5)
f
Fm Ab9 Db9 Db° C7(-5) Fm Ab9 Db9 Db° C° Bbm Bbm7
Bbm(6) Am(6) Fm(6) A9(-5) D9(-5) G9(-5) C7(-5) C7(-5) Fm
f
ff
3

GUITAR
III
Serenade
Creamily (♩ = 63)
A
8
4
Ebm7 Ebm6 F°
E6 F#9 Amaj7 F7(-5)
mf
E6 G#m7 Amaj7 B7(-9 -5)
E6 E° D#° B7(-9)
B
E6 B7(-9) E6
F#9 F9(-5)
mf
E9 Amaj7 A6
B7(-9) E
Abm7 Db(-9)
Gb6 Gb°
Db E♮°
Ebm7 D7(-5)
C
Db Ebm Fm Em
Ebm C Cb
mp
Fm C Db
Ebm Eb9 Abaug9
Db C Cb
Bb Bb° Ebm7
Ab9 Ab9(-5)
Db Ebm Fm Em
D
Ebm7 Ebm6 F°
E6 F#9 Amaj7 B7(-5)
mf
E6 B7(-9) E6
mp
Db Ab7(-9) Db6 Db°
2
close to bridge
p
IV
Horn Belt Boogie
Fast (♩ = 168)
G6
f
F#7 G6
G9(6)
C(6) Cmaj7
C9(-5)
A
G6
G#9
D9
Eb9 D9
G6
B
G6
f
G9
C7

C7 G6 G#° D9 D9 D-9
G6 F#° C Bb6 f
Bb6 Bb7 Eb Eb9(-5) D Bb6 B°
F9 F-9 Bb6 E mf (lightly)
Bb7 Eb Bb Bb°
F7 Bb Db7 F F6 Gb6 F6 Gb6 f
F6 Gb6 F6 Gb6 Eb-9 Db9 Eb-9 Db9 Eb-9 Db9 Eb-9 Db9 Gb6 F6 Gb6 Gb6 F6 Gb6
F6 Gb6 F6 Gb6 F6 Gb6 F6 Gb6 G Gb6 F7 Gb6 Gb9(6)
B6 Bmaj7 B9(-5) Gb(6) G° Db9 D9 Db9
Gb(6) H F#6 G6 F#6 G6 F#6 G6 F#6 G6 F#6 G6 F#6 G6 f
F#6 G6 F#7 G7 B7 C7 B7 C7 B7 C7 B7 C7 F#6 G6 F#6 G6 Bm6 G#° Db9 D9 D7
Db9 D9 D7 F#6 G6 Dm7 F#6 G6 Dm7 G9 C6 C9(-5) C9 G(6)
G#° J Am7 D9 D-9 G(6) Dm7
Dm7 G6 dim. p G6 Ab9(-5) G9(-5) ff

Other ensemble and solo music of interest to brass players from Margun

J.S. Bach

Chorale (from *Cantata No. 60)*
set by Gunther Schuller for two trumpets, horn and trombone
One of Bach's most extraordinary chorales and harmonic inventions; used by Alban Berg in his Violin Concerto

J.S. Bach

Prelude No. 22 (from *Well-Tempered Clavier*)
set by Gunther Schuller for two trumpets, two horns and two trombones
One of the highlights of Bach's well-known masterpiece; the key of B-flat minor inspired Bach to some truly incredible harmonic flights which sound even more dramatic on brass instruments

Brass Transcriptions – Trios, quartets, quintets, sextets and septets (comprising trumpet, horn and trombone) by various 15th- and 16th-century composers, set by Gunther Schuller
Brass transcriptions in a variety of ensemble combinations ranging from motets and madrigals by Dufay, Gesualdo and Marenzio to DeRore's profoundly moving Latin Ode (for four trombones)

Louis Dauprat

Sextuor No. 1 for six horns
A brilliant virtuoso excursion for six horns by the Paris Conservatoire's first professor of horn, appointed by no less than Napoleon; great fun to play, range from low C to high g (concert)

Avram David

Sonata, op. 101 for solo horn
A challenging, almost heroic tour-de-force for unaccompanied horn–ingeniously composed so as not to kill off the horn player–by the well-known Boston-based composer

Lucia Dlugoszewski

Space Is a Diamond for solo trumpet
A remarkable exploration of the outer reaches of trumpet technique; composed for and recorded by Gerard Schwarz; published in a handsome, multi-color engraved edition

Tibor Pusztai

Interactions for horn and three percussion
Effective three-movement work for solo horn set against a diverse percussion background

Gunther Schuller

Fanfare for four trumpets and four trombones
A short, functional 1½-minute fanfare in a harmonic style somewhat akin to Messiaen

Perpetuum Mobile for four muted horns and bassoon (or tuba)
A light-hearted bagatelle in the manner of a Poulenc or Bozza

Trois Hommages for horn(s) and piano
1. À Frederick Delius 2. À Maurice Ravel 3. À Darius Milhaud
Early vintage Schuller, dedicated to three of his youthful influences; accessible, attractive recital and teaching pieces

Robert Selig

Variations for brass quintet
A challenging and difficult single-movement quintet by this dynamic Boston composer

Alec Wilder

Brass Quintets Nos. 1-8

Effie Joins a Carnival for tuba and brass quartet

Elegy for tuba and brass ensemble

Nonet for eight horns and tuba
One of Wilder's finest works: eight horns and tuba in four jazz settings

Sonata for bass trombone and piano

Suites Nos. 1-5 for tuba and piano

Suites Nos. 1 & 2 for horn, tuba and piano

Ellen Taaffe Zwilich

Clarino Quartet for piccolo trumpet, D trumpet and two B-flat trumpets
Brilliant tour-de-force for trumpets in three movements; range from low F to high f (concert)

BASS

Alec Wilder

JAZZ SUITE

for Horn Quartet, Harpsichord, Guitar,
Bass and Drums

I. Horns O'Plenty

II. Conversation Piece

III. Serenade

IV. Horn Belt Boogie

MARGUN MUSIC INC.

167 Dudley Road Newton Centre Massachusetts 02159

BASS

JAZZ SUITE

I
Horns O'Plenty

Alec Wilder

F
f
G
ff
H
mf
f
J
f
K
L
f dim. poco a poco
pp
f sub.
ff

BASS

II
Conversation Piece

BASS
H
J
f
f
ff
III
Serenade
Creamily (♩= 63)
pizz.
mp
p
A
B
mf
C
mp
D
f
mf
arco
p

IV
Horn Belt Boogie

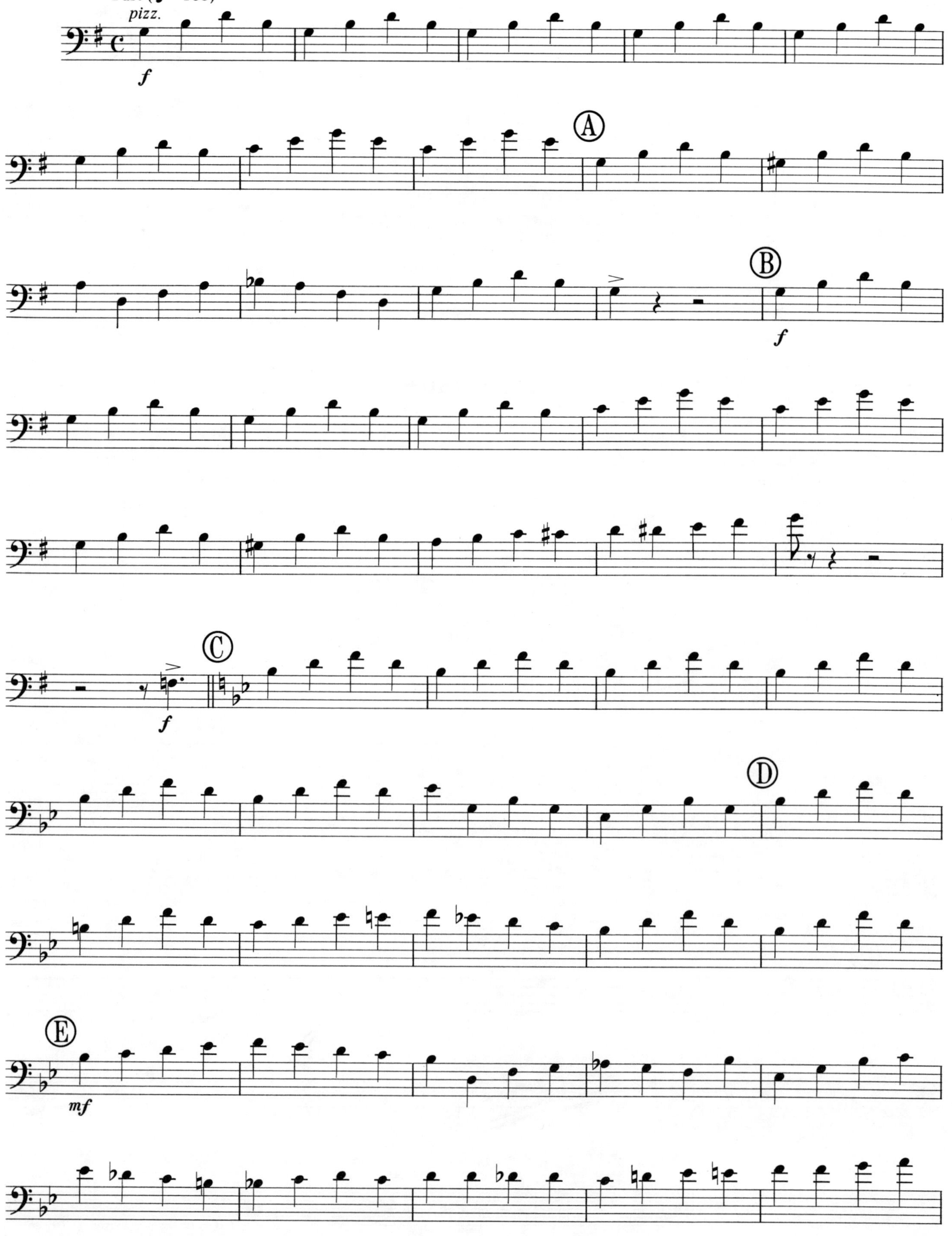

F
f
G
H
f
J
dim.
arco
p
ff

JAZZ SUITE

DRUMS

I
Horns O'Plenty

Alec Wilder

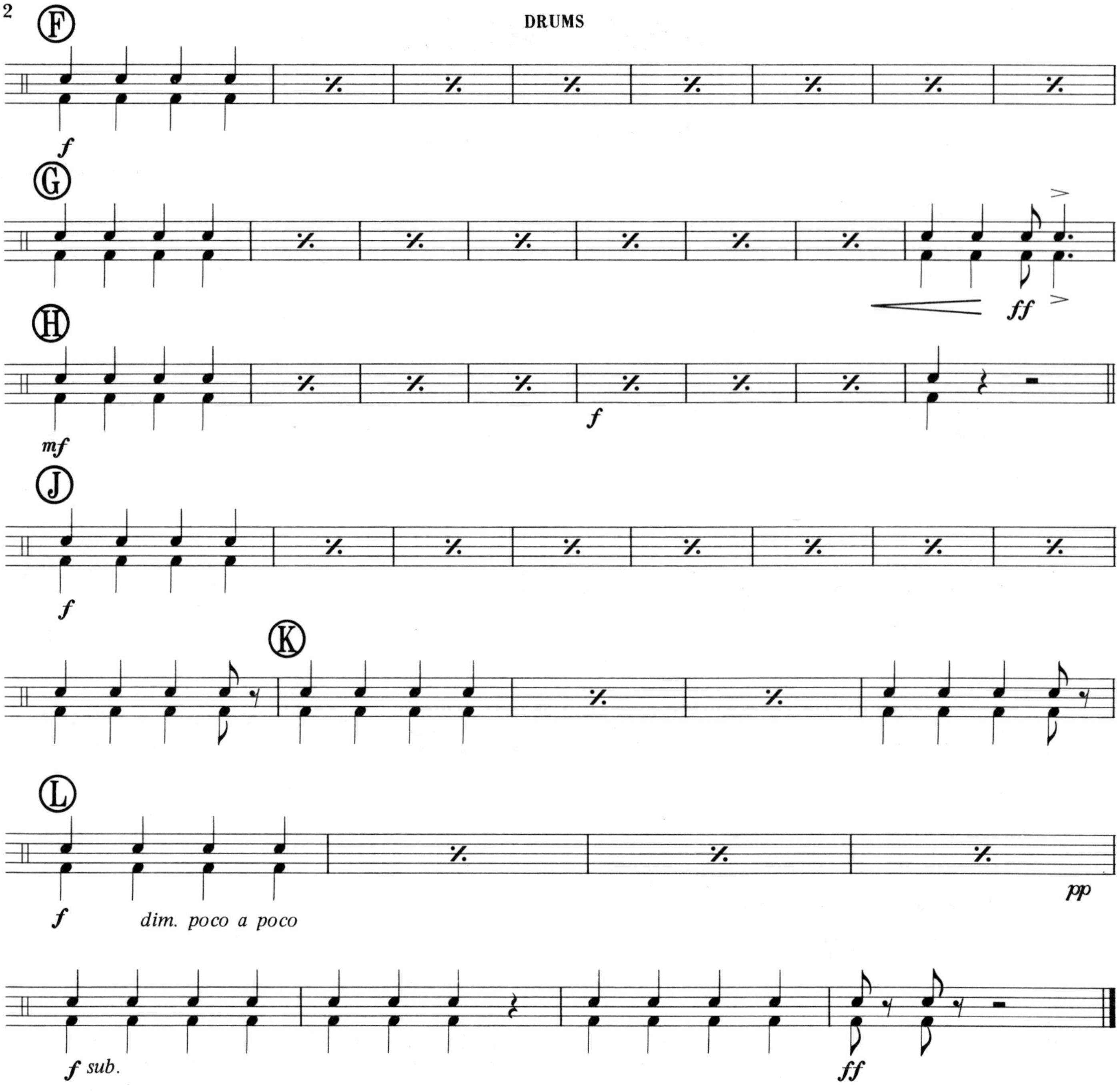
F
f
G
ff
H
mf
f
J
f
K
L
f
dim. poco a poco
pp
f sub.
ff

II
Conversation Piece

Medium Tempo (♩ = 126)
brushes
3
mf
A

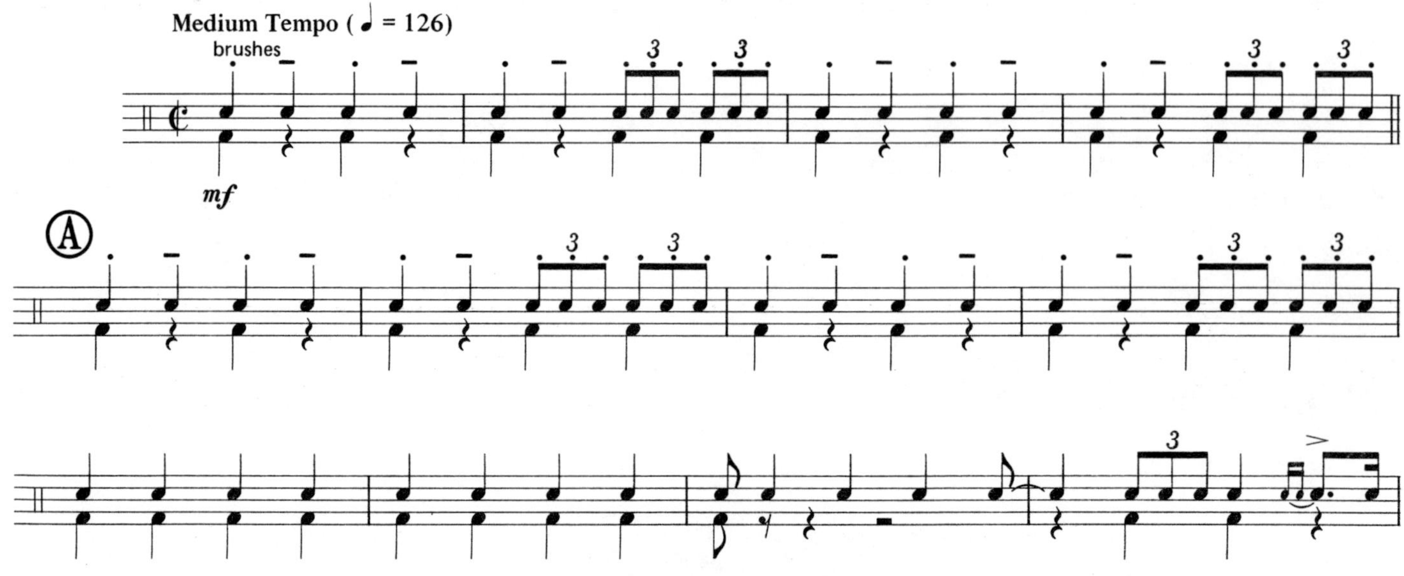

B
mp
C
mf
D
E
F
mp
G
H
J
f
3
f
ff

III
Serenade

Creamily (♩ = 63)

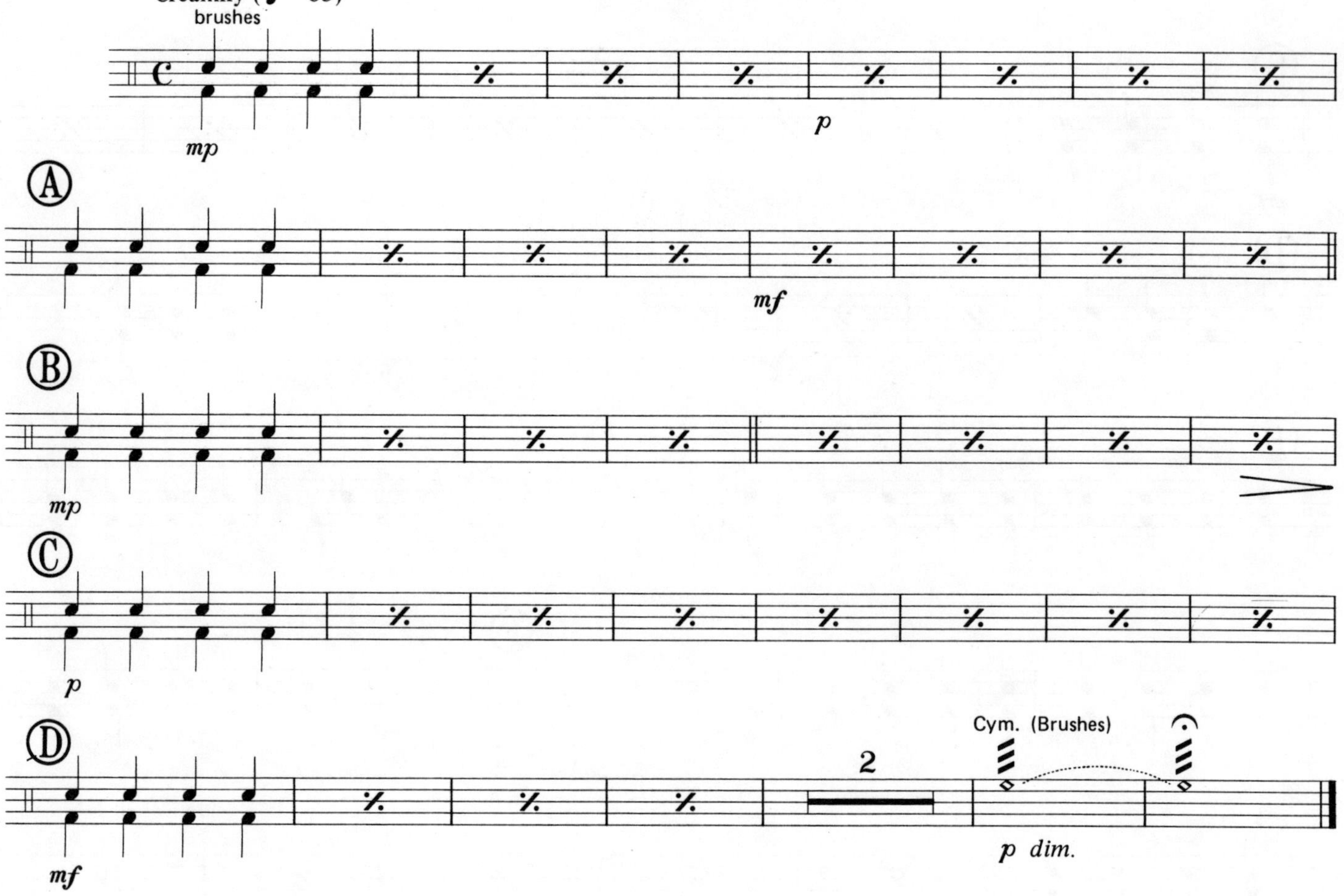
brushes
mp
p
A
mf
B
mp
C
p
D
mf
2
Cym. (Brushes)
p dim.

IV
Horn Belt Boogie

Fast (♩ = 168)

brushes
f
A
B
f
f

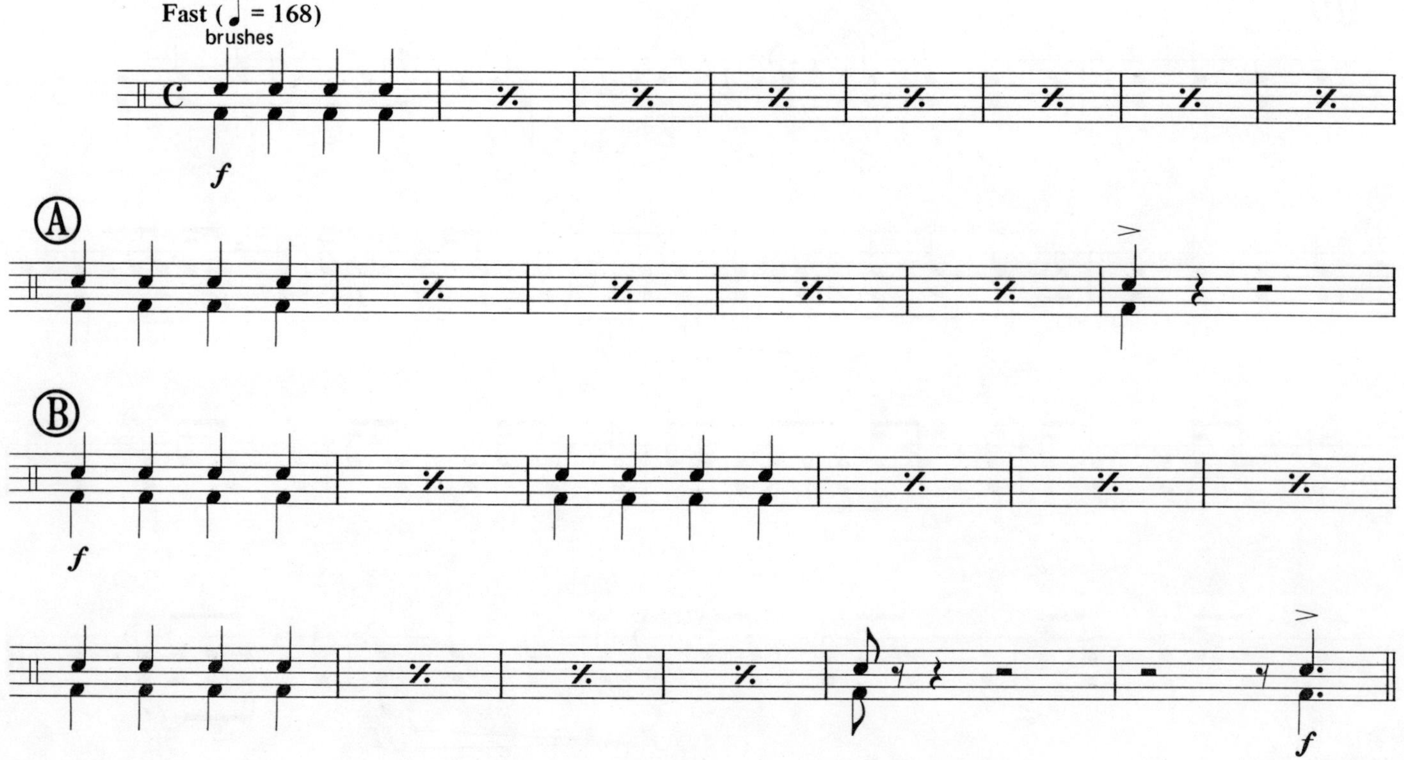

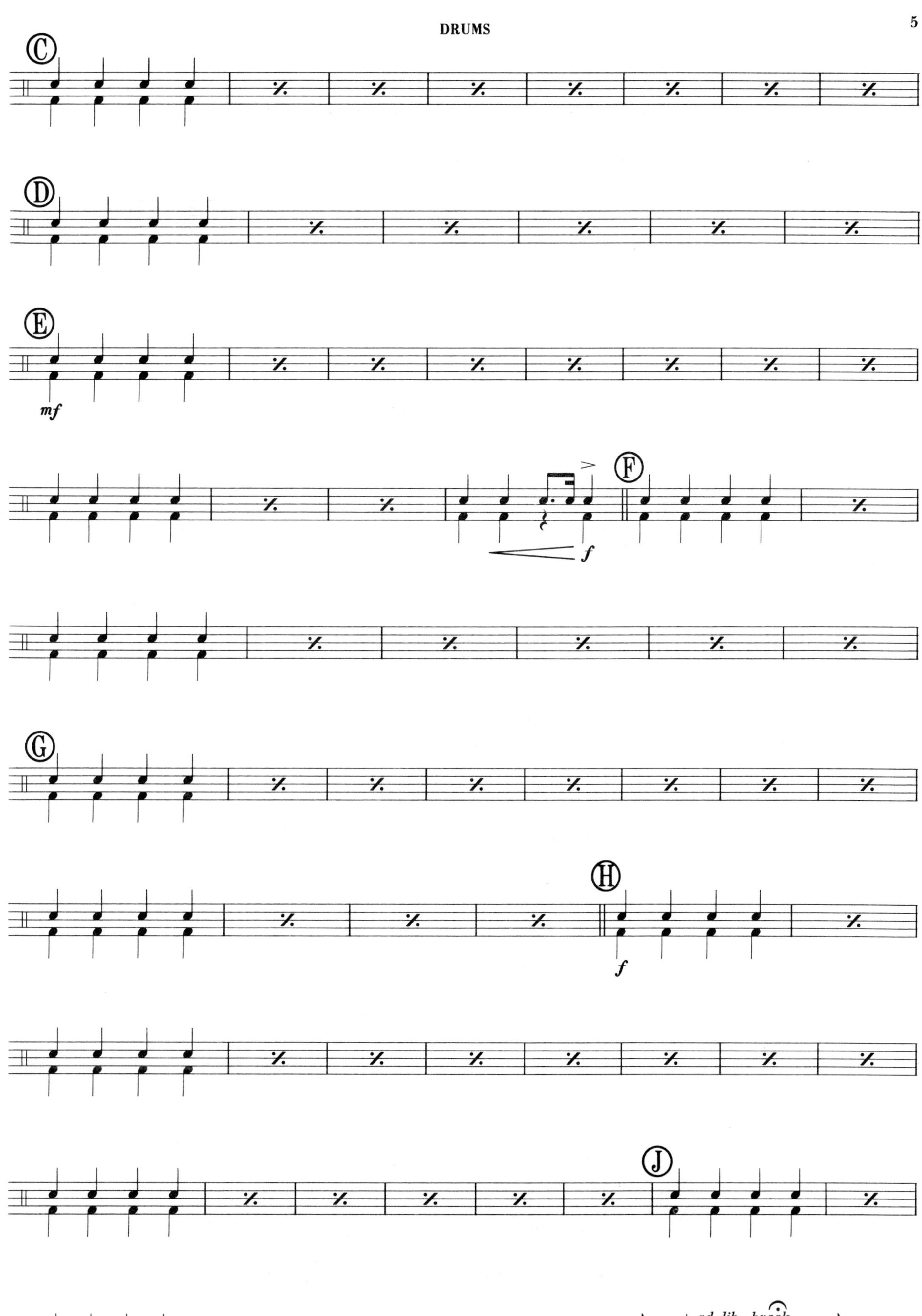
C
D
E
mf
F
f
G
H
f
J
ad lib. break
dim.
p
f

Other ensemble and solo music of interest to brass players from Margun

J.S. Bach	***Chorale*** (from *Cantata No. 60)* set by Gunther Schuller for two trumpets, horn and trombone One of Bach's most extraordinary chorales and harmonic inventions; used by Alban Berg in his Violin Concerto
J.S. Bach	***Prelude No. 22*** (from *Well-Tempered Clavier*) set by Gunther Schuller for two trumpets, two horns and two trombones One of the highlights of Bach's well-known masterpiece; the key of B-flat minor inspired Bach to some truly incredible harmonic flights which sound even more dramatic on brass instruments
	Brass Transcriptions – Trios, quartets, quintets, sextets and septets (comprising trumpet, horn and trombone) by various 15th- and 16th-century composers, set by Gunther Schuller Brass transcriptions in a variety of ensemble combinations ranging from motets and madrigals by Dufay, Gesualdo and Marenzio to DeRore's profoundly moving Latin Ode (for four trombones)
Louis Dauprat	***Sextuor No. 1*** for six horns A brilliant virtuoso excursion for six horns by the Paris Conservatoire's first professor of horn, appointed by no less than Napoleon; great fun to play, range from low C to high g (concert)
Avram David	***Sonata,*** op. 101 for solo horn A challenging, almost heroic tour-de-force for unaccompanied horn–ingeniously composed so as not to kill off the horn player–by the well-known Boston-based composer
Lucia Dlugoszewski	***Space Is a Diamond*** for solo trumpet A remarkable exploration of the outer reaches of trumpet technique; composed for and recorded by Gerard Schwarz; published in a handsome, multi-color engraved edition
Tibor Pusztai	***Interactions*** for horn and three percussion Effective three-movement work for solo horn set against a diverse percussion background
Gunther Schuller	***Fanfare*** for four trumpets and four trombones A short, functional 1½-minute fanfare in a harmonic style somewhat akin to Messiaen
	Perpetuum Mobile for four muted horns and bassoon (or tuba) A light-hearted bagatelle in the manner of a Poulenc or Bozza
	Trois Hommages for horn(s) and piano 1. À Frederick Delius 2. À Maurice Ravel 3. À Darius Milhaud Early vintage Schuller, dedicated to three of his youthful influences; accessible, attractive recital and teaching pieces
Robert Selig	***Variations*** for brass quintet A challenging and difficult single-movement quintet by this dynamic Boston composer
Alec Wilder	***Brass Quintets Nos. 1-8***
	Effie Joins a Carnival for tuba and brass quartet
	Elegy for tuba and brass ensemble
	Nonet for eight horns and tuba One of Wilder's finest works: eight horns and tuba in four jazz settings
	Sonata for bass trombone and piano
	Suites Nos. 1-5 for tuba and piano
	Suites Nos. 1 & 2 for horn, tuba and piano
Ellen Taaffe Zwilich	***Clarino Quartet*** for piccolo trumpet, D trumpet and two B-flat trumpets Brilliant tour-de-force for trumpets in three movements; range from low F to high f (concert)